i

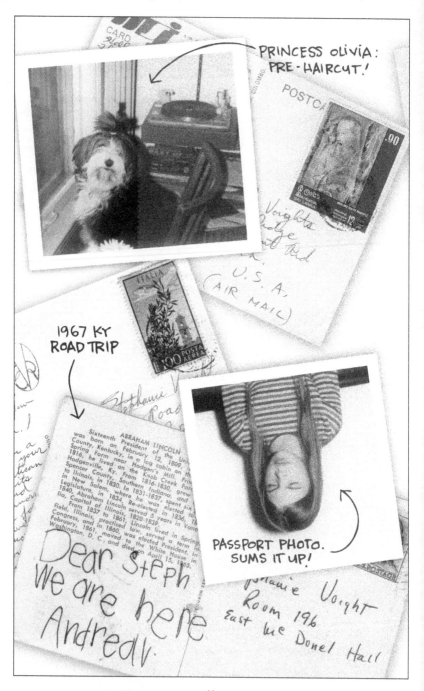

PRINCESS OLIVIA: PRE-HAIRCUT!

1967 KY ROAD TRIP

PASSPORT PHOTO. SUMS IT UP!

MY HANDWRITING
HASN'T IMPROVED

COME TO BERMUDA
THE ISLES OF *Bermuda* POST CARD

Hi Gang.
We're having
a nice TIME.
a waiter! I have
my friend. Its hot
Hi O!ien
Love Annie and

DUBROVNIK

FOOD TO GO

店 飯 園 華

WAH YUEN RESTAURANT
FINE CHINESE FOOD

LOS ANGELES, CALIF. 90012
(NEW CHINA TOWN)

1983 - KEPT IT
ALL THESE YEARS!

MOM ON THE
WAY TO CEYLON!

The PAN AM ONE is the Flagship
It goes around the world. No
complaints I will have had 7 meals
by the time I hit Dehli. Tokyo
And Hong Kong. the runways are
almost in the water - the plane
hits straight down with a thud
otherwise gold be in the water. The
Hong Kong Harbor is beautiful like
Free drinks Hong Kong to Tokyo.
of the women I am taking care of
chairman of Board of Directors-Finance
has asked me to be a guest in
you should see his wife and a kiss
1800 to bring $9000 to buy
aboard one way $9000 to buy
a lovely family Annie take the $$
him we had 3 menu to order

MY NIECE: FUTURE TRAIN LOVER

Cover photos:

Top photo: Dubrovnik, Yugoslavia
Middle photo: Hudson Valley area in New York.
Bottom photo: Brother Brad somewhere in Nevada.

Traveling with Family

Traveling with Family

A memoir of sorts

Written by Andrea Voight
Illustrations & cover by Pamela G. Jones

Publishing by Doodlestreet

Text and photos copyright © 2015 by Andrea Voight.
Illustrations copyright © 2015 by Pamela G. Jones.
All rights reserved. Published by Doodlestreet.

ISBN number: 978-1511485401.
First Edition.
Printed by CreateSpace, An Amazon.com Company.

Available from Amazon.com and other online stores ~
Search the author's name, Andrea Voight.

Dedication

To my parents, two of a kind; to my brothers and sisters, all great traveling companions; and to Olivia and Pup, the two best traveling dogs ever.

And to Sweet Pea, also a great traveler, and for assistance with this "masterpiece." ....

Contents

Chapter One

Introduction of Characters

Namely my parents. They loved traveling the world, especially on a moment's notice. They were also fortunate to have traveled during the glamour days of ocean liners, when you didn't have 3,500 people fighting for food at the buffet and when trains were dominant throughout the United States. We were very fortunate they would take us kids with them on trips.

When you have a large family, however, not everyone is able to travel together. I think they tried that a few times when I was very young and thankfully I don't recall anything. I was traumatized enough by our travels later in life and didn't need any searing childhood memories, such as being told about having a rash and not being allowed to board a ship, or driving through the night on our way to Florida, hoping the car didn't break down in the back woods. Was I even born yet? With so many bodies piled into the car it was probably impossible to tell if they left anyone behind.

Growing up in suburban Detroit made traveling easier. Access to airports, trains, lakes and freeways paved the way to many great adventures to all points in the U.S. and Canada. Missing of course in the 1960s, 70s and 80s were the internet, cell phones and comfortable chain hotels. What we would have given for complimentary breakfasts and kids-eat-free bargains that are ubiquitous today when on the road.

Not that my parents were spendthrifts, (I confess, they were to some degree) but you just didn't know what hotel or motel you'd find -- if any -- until you stumbled into a town at night. No toll-free hotel numbers back then. No trip reviews. Plus motels usually charged per kid. Great. As the youngest I always feared being left in the car. So with a large family and appetite for traveling, my parents had to cut costs whenever possible.

Car camping wasn't all that bad. One gets used to sleeping in the back seat or across a thin board propped on top of seats in the roomy station wagons of yesteryear. Bench seats were great, too. But for some reason our cars got smaller as us kids grew taller.

The interstate rest areas in those days were also great sleepover spots for many travelers, mainly us. Too bad we didn't know about the free coffee and cookies that you can still find at rest stops in Oregon and Washington. I guarantee you we would have driven coast-to-coast every summer just for those tidbits.

When it came to food, my mom would bring loaves of French or dark rye bread, sharp cheddar cheese and Thermoses of coffee. If we were well-behaved, we got those tiny boxes of cereal, too. She also brought milk. There was always the half gallon of warm skim milk taken from the home refrigerator as to not waste it by leaving it there to expire. I can't count the times I heard in the car, "We need to drink up this milk."

My dad usually ignored all the squabbling until of course you heard the magic words, "Don't make me stop this car and throw you out." Luckily for us he had a great sense of humor, which matched my mother's dry sense of humor, which matched our muttly shaggy dog's sense of humor, which came in handy during one road trip south.

The three of us were headed to my college in Texas

when my mother suddenly decided to trim our dog's hair in the back seat. Olivia, our dog, just rolled with it. My dad and I said nothing as we heard the occasional 'yip' followed by fur flying around inside the car as we couldn't open the windows because of the hot, humid rainy conditions outside.

My dad, a human GPS, loved to be the driver. It was our job to keep him awake during long road trips because whenever we asked him how he was doing he'd always reply with snoring. But what do you expect from a man who wanted to attach a surfboard atop his red, compact car in winter and go to our suburban fast-food drive-thru? You'd expect the same from him when at a red light, a neighboring car would be blasting the latest urban rap song, so my dad would quickly find the song on the car radio, roll down *his* windows and suddenly it was stereo-surround sound at the stoplight.

He had timeless wisdom when it came to traveling:
1) The same kid kicking my dad's seat has been behind him on every plane and train trip.
2) No matter how empty the hotel swimming pool, families will always swim into your corner of the pool.
3) Never trust a 25 cent lightbulb, meaning never trust another car's blinking turn signal.

Introduction of Characters

Thankfully my dad didn't have a temper with us kids coming and going out of the car during our numerous trips. I really appreciated that as an adult when we were leaving our Michigan house bright and early to travel east. Remember those 5 a.m. wake-up calls in the dark? "Let's go!" I fondly recall stumbling to the car and, once inside, falling into a blissful sleep against the window while my dad drove. But I digress.

As we left the driveway on this muggy, summer morning I wondered, now where did I put those three cans of pop? The answer came driving down the street when the soda cans crashed onto the windshield one by one and rolled off the car. I'm just glad it wasn't a new car.

Anyone who travels has good, bad and horror stories to share. These are a few of mine, to the best of my recollections, Your Honor.

Chapter Two

Detroit to Mexico City, summer 1970

Where do I even begin with this jaunt? Whenever anyone at my job mentioned their worst trip, mine was always the hands-down winner followed by dropped jaws. All I had to say: "We took a bus home from Mexico City to Detroit."

I was 9 years old and don't remember too much of the trip's beginning. The rest of it though I've never forgotten. My mother, sister, brother and I were traveling by train from Detroit to visit new acquaintances who lived in Mexico City. Also on the agenda was Veracruz, Mexico, but alas, we never made it there.

My memories of this trip pick up in the Mexican border town of Nuevo Laredo. Back then you were implored to never drink the water in Mexico. I drank the water. Yes, right from the fountain outside the train station. These were the days before bottled water or free soda drink refills. I zeroed in on that water fountain like a fighter pilot. I couldn't help but drink because it was so hot and dusty outside. The water was cold and free. Ahhhhh. After my quick slurps I wandered alone in front of the station, chitchatting with some teen boys, until I was intercepted by my frantic mother. See what happens when you travel with more than one kid?

Then it was back on the train, this time, a Mexican-run train. It didn't bother me that we were riding in coach with the open windows, wooden seats and farmers carrying their caged roosters. The countryside filled with cacti was a pleasant change from the Midwest. But I guess it really bothered my mother because she had paid for train compartments with beds that were supposedly attached to the same train. After some discussion with some conductor, we gathered our things and wandered back to our sleeper car.

My mother always had a big heart for the poorer kids in the Mexican villages. She had traveled several times to Mexico with other kids in our family and always brought bags of clothes and candy to give to children outside the train doors. I remember on this trip giving kids candy and sweaters. Leave it to my mom to bring sweaters in summer.

So far, so good. The Nuevo Laredo drinking water episode hadn't become reality. I was getting along with my older brother and my sister was teaching me Spanish soundbites. We also met on the train a newlywed couple from Louisiana who became our new best friends during this vacation because they had never left Louisiana and were rather intimidated by a foreign land. They are probably still talking about us or at least the bus ride home. But hey, they only had to go to Louisiana.

We finally arrived in Mexico City. I remember seeing the lights of downtown and this time drinking numerous bottles of apple soda. *¡Delicioso!* We even went to a bullfight. Our hotel room was nice and while it didn't include free breakfast, it did include the Louisianans in the next room. I don't know if they had a different hotel, but suddenly there were six of us traveling together. Who knows what their parents thought of them hanging out in Mexico City during their honeymoon with a mom and her three kids from Detroit?

I remember visiting the pyramids, climbing the Sun pyramid twice. No fears when you're a kid. We found the Zócalo; we prayed on our knees in front of the massive Cathedral; and more importantly we discovered Sanborns Department store and their delicious ice cream sundaes. I think we even found a Woolworths, great for breakfasts.

Simple beginnings to the trip. Soon to change. We later met our friends - a father and the oldest son - who lived in the city. My middle brother met the son while sailing aboard the R.M.S. *Queen Elizabeth* from Europe. Blah, blah, blah. The son also visited our family in Detroit, and likewise my brother went to see him in Mexico City. At age 11 or so. Alone on a nonstop flight from Detroit where he experienced *jalapeño* peppers before anyone else in our family and was quite sorry he did.

Anyway, the son and his dad showed us (minus the Louisianans) around their home in the Federal District within Mexico City. After that quick tour, they announced we were all going to drive down to Cuernavaca to see their summer home and meet the rest of their family. Nevermind we were supposed to go to Veracruz by ourselves. But when in Rome ... err, Mexico City.

The only problem was nobody told the mother we were coming to Cuernavaca. Not sure how that slipped through the cracks. No cell phones to call ahead. The only other problem was the ride in the mountains to their house. The dad liked to race cars in Europe. THANKS. I was so carsick. Probably from the twist and turns along the highway, or sadly it could have been from passing a person who laid dead in the road after being hit by a car. Someone had even put a bucket over the deceased's head.

We finally made it in one piece to Cuernavaca to this family's beautiful, sprawling ranch house surrounded by lush greenery. Now I never recall getting any food or drink out of this deal, probably just as well considering, but you'd think driving and traveling all this way through the Mexican countryside that we would get something to eat?

My mom's first clue things were going awry was when the nervous mother greeted us, with not so much as a hello, but some wisecrack about how her children didn't look like the other kids in Mexico. Say what? Needless to say, we only stayed a few hours then it was back to Mexico City to our hotel and our newylweds.

Chapultepec Park would be our last foray into the city. You know it's better to start these excursions in the morning, giving you plenty of daylight to make it back to your hotel. Luckily the Louisianans were with us. Safety in numbers.

I'm not going to brag about having street smarts, even at 9 years old, but it does help to have them in your back pocket when your family and your newlyweds are alone on a city bus with some weirdo guy trying to sell you watches. Unfortunately the newlywed husband didn't know too much about men trying to sell watches in a park.

It was getting dark when we were nearing a remote area of the park. This guy wanted us to exit the bus and go with him into the park to see these "watches." As a kid, my watch was always asking my dad what time was it? I didn't need to see any in a park in a foreign city.

Our bus driver, of course, was oblivious and didn't offer any words of discouragement. I think the newlywed husband was halfway off the bus with the weirdo watch-man when the newlywed wife and all of us told him, "This isn't such a good idea." The newlywed husband relented and returned to his seat.

Then I remember the famous words uttered angrily -- yet in perfect English -- by this weirdo watch-man as he stepped off the bus, "Things will be different in the morning." Yikes! Of course by now the watch-man knew the hotel where we were staying, and for all I can remember, probably the names of the newlyweds' relatives, cats, dogs, goats, etc.

Fear and panic followed. My mom was concerned enough to discuss safety strategies with the front-desk clerks at our hotel. The next thing I knew we were in our room, blocking the door with mattresses and chairs. We just had to make it through the night. I'm sure glad we had prayed earlier that week at the Cathedral.

We made it through the night. Now for going home. The newlyweds decided to leave with us. Hmmmm. We were supposed to depart for home on the train. Emphasis on the "supposed to." Yet for some reason, and who knows why, our train reservations were messed up. Or the train employees were on strike. Or the train was broken. So now what? You knew we weren't going to spend real money and fly home. No.

We took the bus.

And guess what? The newlyweds took the bus with us! So now this vagabond group was heading home on a bus through the Mexican countryside. This mode of transportation took a tad longer than the train and had no air conditioning or bathrooms on board, so naturally once you learn that, all bets are off.

And so were my pants at one point. Let me explain.

My bathroom urge hit the first day traveling through rancho country. Maybe in the first hour. Really bad. My mom didn't know what to do. She tried to get the bus driver to stop, but he spoke zero English. Where was my older sister and her Spanish soundbites? The newlywed husband tried to get me to think of anything other than needing the bathroom. Nothing was helping. I'm sure my brother was getting a kick out of this. I don't think he drank the entire trip.

Now my bladder was about to explode. The bus driver stopped in the middle of nowhere, letting my mom and me off the bus. Luckily for my bladder there was a white rancho house in a field near the deserted highway.

My mom and I raced through the cacti- and snake-filled terrain. We knocked on the rancho door and the young family opening it looked at us like we were from Mars. They actually let us in, but I'm sure they changed the locks once we left. My mom tried to explain we needed to use their bathroom. Again, no *comprende*. But when you think about it, wouldn't most folks think bathroom first when a mom and her kid show up un-announced at your rancho front door?

Then my mom started to pull down my pants to make a language barrier visual. Sigh.

I'm not sure what the couple thought of that. The next thing I remember we were back out in the field and I'm squatting and, well, you get the picture. (So did everyone on the bus.) Why didn't we use the field in the first place? Oh, I know, because of the cacti and looming snakes. And where was my sister and her Spanish soundbites? Didn't anyone know "*baño?*"

At least the bus driver waited for us. He was sure a lot nicer than the bus driver at the park. We climbed back on board. I didn't care if everyone was staring at me, I was just glad to be relieved of my previous situation. The next situation occurred when the newlyweds approached us with the brilliant idea of taking us home to their goat ranch in western Louisiana. Why not? Nothing else on this trip had gone to schedule. We never made it to Veracruz, but I doubt we had hotel reservations. A cancellation fee was never mentioned.

So now it was off to the newlyweds' goat ranch. We must have picked up another bus or car ride from San Antonio to Louisiana. I can't remember. The traveling started to blend together by this time. The newlyweds' parents were just as surprised as our Mexican friends to see a mom and her three kids suddenly show up at their goat ranch.

But Southern hospitality came through and we stayed a few days which included a throwdown, I mean, barbecue. The baby goats were very cute and playful and hopefully not part of the menu that evening. I also tried homemade banana ice cream. All interesting tastes and great fun until the Nuevo Laredo water episode kicked in. And it did with a bang there in western Louisiana. Needless to say I was glad we were finally going home to Michigan. We said our good-byes to the newlyweds as they dropped us off at the bus station. This bus had bathrooms. Woo-hoo! I don't remember much about the trip from there, other than waking up hot and dizzy in St. Louis, seeing the Gateway Arch and eating pancakes somewhere.

And then like that, it was over. At least my dad knew to pick us up at the bus station in downtown Detroit and not the train station. And he knew better not to ask us why we weren't on the train.

Chapter Three

Bermuda, September 1970

A last-minute trip, just my dad and me, aboard the Greek cruise ship S.S. *Olympia*. A very small ship by today's standards as I was the only kid on board. Of course it was the start of the school year so that explains that. This ship had none of the theme park amenities like the cruise liners of today. This was old school. Only one pool, the size of a refrigerator box, and filled with icy salt water. On-deck entertainment? Shuffleboard.

The ship was leaving from New York harbor, but first we had to get there. My dad wanted to fly, but I was scared to fly even though I'd never flown. So it was the train to Penn Station. You would have thought I had sworn off trains after Mexico City. We arrived in Manhattan and spent the day sightseeing around the city before boarding our ship at night. Once on board and after the midnight buffet, I was off to bed. The next morning I felt a little queasy but nothing ginger ale wouldn't cure.

It was the middle of hurricane season. Maybe some of our vacations were taken at odd times of the year when greater discounts were given. Had to cut costs somewhere. I was very excited to be at sea and of course, not in school. I left our dungeon of a room and wandered the deck alone and as long as you didn't fall overboard, nobody cared.

I found my dad on deck but my spirits quickly waned as the first thing I saw were twin waterspouts in the near distance. I had always been afraid of storms and tornadoes and now I was getting a close-up view of the waterspouts dancing off the water. I think I hit the bar after that, ordering my favorite ginger ale with cherries. Luckily we skirted the storms and made it to Bermuda and back unscathed. On the trip home my dad and I were fortunate to dine at the Captain's table where I was very grateful that my long hair didn't catch on fire from the flaming Baked Alaska.

Chapter Four

Dubrovnik, Yugoslavia, spring 1973

Some people were lucky enough to take a plane trip when they were kids, usually to familiar places like Washington, D.C., or New York City.

My first plane trip oddly enough was to Dubrovnik, Yugoslavia. Who knew you could even fly there from Detroit? We did. On Saturn Airlines (funny, our family later owned plenty of Saturn cars). This time I was joined by my Dad, sister and brother.

We said good-bye to my siblings and my mom, but not before she cut locks of our hair. I wondered what she knew that we didn't?

This trip went without any big hitch. I remember the

delicious ice cream, huge oranges for a nickel (1 *dinar*), the walled city and playing ping-pong at the hotel. More bus rides, too. This time from the hotel into the city on winding, hilly roads that should have been condemned. Glad I still have these memories because my dad maybe took five pictures of the entire trip. What's up with that!? Too bad we didn't have digital cameras.

We were served Croatian food on the plane trip home. I drank a lot of milk when I was a kid, so I asked for some, thinking it would come in a nice little carton. Instead, but not complaining here, it was goat's milk that came in a tall glass, complete with a layer of skin on top. I had no idea our Louisiana goats were also providing beverages for this airline.

At least my sister taught me soundbites of the Croatian language. Comes in handy today when you're trying to avoid weirdos on buses or subways.

Chapter Five

'But officer...' New England, summer 1974-ish?

There is nothing like summer in the The Hamptons. Of course, we never traveled there, but we did to Hampton Beach, N.H., and that was for only one night.

My oldest brothers and sisters spent many summers when they were younger at camps in Rhode Island and near Cape Cod, Mass. I made some of these East Coast treks along Highway 401 through Ontario, the Massachusetts Turnpike and the New York State Thruway, where visions of Ted's Hot Dogs still come to mind.

I don't remember how many summers we did this. The only thing I clearly remember was a 1974-ish trip traveling in our brown, sporty two-door. Did I mention it was a two-door? Maybe meant for two people comfortably and not five? This time it was my parents, two brothers and me (all of us kids tall).

It was August when we started this trip down memory lane. We arrived late afternoon in Boston, unaware of a hurricane winding its way up the East Coast. No 24-hour weather programs on TV or fancy weather web sites to save us from the impending doom.

Our rooms at our downtown Boston hotel were given away and no other rooms were available because folks were coming to the city to avoid the storm. On a different note, one might ask, if we could afford this somewhat fancy hotel in downtown Boston why didn't we always stay at these in other cities? I think we may have been stockholders in the hotel chain, but I have no idea why the extremes. If we weren't sleeping at these hotels, we were sleeping in the car.

So where does a carload of five look for accommodations when Boston is out of rooms? New Hampshire. We were off, driving up the coast past picturesque Marblehead, Mass. That was on our left side. The choppy ocean and ominous dark clouds were on our right side. I avoided looking right as I was still highly afraid of storms. No motels or hotels along the road, and if there were, it was no vacancy. Now it was getting late. Thankfully we didn't hear much complaining or swearing from my dad. He left all that behind in Boston.

Besides the excitement one feels from the negative ions of an approaching storm, I was also excited because now we were crossing state lines into New Hampshire, a new state for me! My mom suddenly remembered Hampton Beach being a touristy town, so maybe we would have luck finding a motel room. We arrived around 9 p.m. It was almost 11 p.m. when we found a room. And one room it was. In a boarding house. Great view of the beach, so they said. We later discovered the beach, a hard six blocks from the boarding house.

Fitting five people into a room meant for two-and-a-half takes some thinking. My older brother didn't think too long and bolted for the luxury of our sporty two-door, parked in front of the boarding house.

The rest of us were stuck in the cheaply paneled room crammed with bunk beds, a small desk and chair, and a lightbulb hanging overhead. Looked just like a cell block. No bathroom, either. Again with the bathroom. We had to cross the living room, bypassing these strangers and their blaring TV, to use the facilities. Luckily our room was so hot that any liquid inside of us evaporated, thus squelching the need for the bathroom.

Sleep is overrated. I think it was 4 a.m. when my other brother opted out of the room for some battered couch on the cooler front porch. The boys were allowed but the *girls weren't.* So I was banished to the sweat lodge.

All was bliss until the Sunday morning wake-up call from police yelling outside. My porch brother quickly returned and we watched from the only window - stupid when you think about it, possible gunfire. There were several officers and police cars blocking the street. A drug bust or robbery or something was going down. Policemen were standing by our sporty two-door where my brother was still asleep until he popped up his head like a dog looking for its owner. Instead he found policemen who were just as surprised to see him.

Luckily my brother wasn't shot or hauled in for questioning back in our boarding house room on the chair under the light. "Why were you sleeping in the car when there are perfectly good rooming houses with bunk beds available?" ... "But officer, there are five of us in a room meant for two-and-a-half."

With no court dates or bail hearings, we left New Hampshire behind. Next stop? Maine. It was on this highway to who-knows-where in Maine that my fondness for inanimate objects began.

I was in the back seat (next to my two big brothers) pressed against the door, trying to sleep with my head resting on a small, flowered couch pillow. I shouldn't have rolled down the window all the way for the next thing I knew my little pillow fell out of the car. I was horrified as I looked out the rear window, watching my little pillow roll behind us into the distance. I cried out to my dad to turn the car around, but he adamantly refused. Not for a pillow. A kid, maybe. But not a pillow. My brothers teased me, saying my little pillow was probably crying now that it was all alone on the road. I would have hit them right then and there if we had more room in the back seat. To this day I can still see my little pillow on the road. The trauma.

Speaking of traumatic experiences. ... We found some when we stayed at a bed-and-breakfast somewhere near the Maine coast. There weren't many motels along that stretch of coastline, but the B&B industry was starting to flourish.

The house we found from a road sign was white and rambling with plenty of huge trees in the front yard and access to a very muddy beach along a bay in the back yard. We stayed two days. One day too long. We must have been this couple's first ever house guests. They were probably hoping for a young, newlywed couple (we should have sent them the Louisianans), but were stuck with this motley crew of us five. From Michigan. We could barely understand their accents and likewise with ours.

The couple, who had about three kids and a rather large dog, were gracious at first but then quickly went over the rules. The do's and don'ts. I mean, come on people, it's not like we just left prison. Well, we kind of did after that boarding house. One of the big no-no's was food in their house. The only food allowed was to be what they served us in the morning. Maybe they didn't want food particles on the wooden floors, crumbs in the beds or water marks on the antique furniture. It was their house, so you do what your told. So what if we had to wait until breakfast to eat?

Are you kidding me? Teenagers eat around the clock. The 'no-food regulation' wouldn't have been a problem except there wasn't anywhere to eat within an hour of this house, excuse me, B&B. We finally found a market/ gas station somewhere but you could only buy groceries and leave. No loitering or eating on the premises or you would probably be shot on the spot.

So being the adventurous family we purchased food and returned to the bed-and-breakfast to break all etiquette laws by sneaking edibles into the house. We forgot about their dog.

My older brother volunteered to smuggle the contraband (ham, cheese and bread), all in a paper bag tucked under his jacket, up the outside back stairs to the porch accessing our room. We waited in the car. We were no fools. That dog wasn't either. I'm sure he was trained just for these occasions.

Sure enough, as my brother was half way up the stairs, the dog scrambled from around the house and confronted him, barking, growling and sniffing his jacket. My brother looked helplessly our way. We waved to him from the safety of the car as we quietly planned our escape route without him just in case.

But we jumped the gun. My brother simply slipped the dog a piece of ham, patted it on the head and the dog left, satisfied. Now we could all sneak up the stairs and dig into the food. Quietly, of course.

We prepared a makeshift kitchen in one of the bathrooms. The empty chest of drawers quickly became a pantry of sorts. No ice machines but thankfully we purchased foods that didn't need refrigeration. My mom was always thinking. Any leftovers (highly unlikely with three teens) would be given to the dog, our new best friend. Good thing we had these sandwiches because the morning "breakfasts" consisted mainly of toast, jam, juice and coffee with the family observing our every move.

Their backyard beach wasn't anything to rave about, either. Just mud and ice-cold water. Oh well, it was a port in a storm and offered a glimpse into the new world of B&Bs. I don't think this couple really knew what to do with us. They probably closed up shop after we left. Maybe opened a restaurant. No dogs allowed. Food, yes. Hopefully you could eat it there as well.

Chapter Six

Las Vegas, June 1975

Plane travel in the 1970s was still rather pricey for a family to be hopping off to places like Las Vegas or Los Angeles or Miami. Plus there were all those pesky hijackings to Cuba (why never Tahiti?). Anyway, we just liked traveling by car. The details of this trip are dark, as most of my memories of it were at night.

I think our dog Olivia was with us. I can't recall. She didn't keep a diary. But I know she did travel with us on one trip west, which included driving past the stockyards in Kansas City where her olfactories went crazy.

Moooooving on (I couldn't resist) ... we left our Detroit home for this road trip - my first one west - just as the summer temps were arriving. My oldest brother had moved to Las Vegas and we took this journey to help him get settled there.

My dad, mom, brother and I left, thinking winter was over, only to have it resurface again while sleeping along the Continental Divide. I'm not talking about the geographical designation, although we were near that because I saw the sign in Wyoming. I'm talking about the cold, metal flap seam that appeared when you folded down the rear seats of a station wagon. That's what my brother and I slept across while my parents were up front as we couldn't find any motel in this remote part of the state. Plus it was frigid outside.

I wish we had brought more blankets for these car excursions. I had many blankets in my car years later when I lived in California in case I had to spend a winter's night stuck on the 710 in Long Beach.

This Las Vegas trip has me puzzled as I remember it being dark all the time. Like for some reason driving over Hoover Dam into Boulder City, Nev., and then Las Vegas. These days Hoover Dam is a mega-tourist attraction. Back then at 11 p.m. it was scary and deserted. I recall the humming of the dam's inner workings and seeing the glowing orange lights as we drove atop it, all reminding me of entering a prison yard.

Las Vegas, June 1975

I wonder if we ever drove anywhere during the daytime? Maybe we drove at night in the desert to avoid the summer heat, and, well really, people in general.

After Vegas and all the $1.99 breakfasts one could tolerate, we took the southern route home to Detroit. My dad would find the classic "The Shadow Knows" program on the car radio as we drove the lonely highways home. That was always fun to hear those scary stories right before sleeping. Luckily for us, our first stop in Winslow, Ariz., consisted of no sleep.

We were in the middle of nowhere and had to park at the small Winslow train station, and you know where there is a train station, there are trains. Lots of them. One every half hour. Complete with blaring horns and the ground rumbling beneath our car. Made me long for another train trip.

Chapter Seven

'One Sandwich Per Person,'
winter 1976-77

Speaking of long train trips, it was my brother's senior year in high school and my parents thought it would be fun to take the train to Las Vegas for an early graduation present. Thankfully they discarded ideas of taking our station wagon again since it was winter.

This was Christmas break when colds and the flu surfaced. I was lucky to avoid those but instead came down with a nasty sinus infection complete with mild fever. I knew we were traveling soon, so I tried to rally and fake not being sick, but my mom wasn't buying it. Especially with a fever. She was a nurse. She thought it best we stayed home.

I heard my mom telling my dad and brother we

should cancel the vacation. She loved calling the train people to find deals, discover new routes, etc. I think my mother spent more time calling them than her own children. Just kidding. Now she was back on the phone to the train people to set the wheels in motion to get a refund.

Then I heard crying.

My head may have been stuffed, but my ears weren't. My 17-year-old brother was tearing up in the dining room. Unbelieveable. So there I was, fading fast on the living room couch, rolling my eyes at his acting performance. My throat hurt too much to object.

But I was relieved we weren't going. I didn't care about his needs. Just mine. Well, we weren't going for about five minutes. My dad felt sorry for my brother. Excuse me?? Hello?? I'm the one with chills and great pain over here on the couch. My dad wanted to make it up to my brother and decided we would still take the trip.

Just as quickly as it had begun, the crying stopped.

I think it was 10 p.m. when my mother finally got us rebooked on *a* train to Las Vegas. But there was a minor problem. The original trip before my costly infection and fever was my family traveling in a comfy sleeper car and taking the direct route through Chicago.

Now suddenly we were going to Las Vegas through New Orleans and El Paso and Los Angeles. In coach. And now suddenly it seemed like I was the bad seed for making this happen. Off we went!

The only good thing about having a sinus infection when you're sitting in coach on a train for days on end is you have to sit upright the entire time, so you're always afforded good sinus drainage. My mother made me drink fluids, mostly hot water. She knew how to care for me on the road. She would plead with the porters for cups of hot water whenever they walked by (wearing their crisp white jackets). At one point I heard a porter muttering, "What does that woman want with all that hot water?" Another time in her quest to find hot water for my dire sinus condition, my mom grabbed the arm of a guy who was walking by and also wearing a white sweater only to be told, "I'm not a porter, lady." Sorry!

There were also the very colorful characters traveling in coach. Not that I wanted to know their backgrounds, but at night I wondered how many had committed crimes and just how heinous were those crimes?

Or you have seat mates who are constantly looking at you to make eye contact so they can ramble on about their life stories.

Then there are those always making noise to get your attention to their plight. This night there was a couple arguing a few rows away from us. Nothing to bring in the police, but enough to irritate some folks, like one woman who would "shush" them every five minutes to get them to shut up. Now this action was keeping everyone else in the car awake. So my dad took it upon himself to "shush" the "shusher." Every time she "shushed" the couple, my dad would "shush" her just as quickly. There was "shushing" ricocheting all over that train.

I made it through that night and the train pulled into New Orleans. I still had no appetite but it didn't stop my parents and brother from gorging on Mexican food at this all-you-can-eat restaurant. Each table had a little flag to raise whenever you wanted refills on food. I'm sure that string broke at some point. But wait, here we were back in Louisiana (we should have called ahead to the newlyweds), home of great seafood and beignets, and we were eating Mexican food?

After our layover in New Orleans, we departed for the long journey west. My fever broke outside El Paso, day three on the train. And I could finally eat a little. French toast. Delicious.

Then it was off to Los Angeles. I remember waking up to the aroma of orange blossoms outside as the train approached San Bernardino. I was so excited to finally see California, thinking I was going to run into Michael Jackson and family. We unloaded at L.A.'s Union Station where I immediately combed through the phone books for "Jackson." I was that pathetic. I even ripped out a few pages, thinking I had found their number.

We ate lunch from the vendor carts on Olvera Street, then it was back on the train for Las Vegas. That was fun when the train descended the mountains and you could see the approaching lights of the city. My Vegas brother would always meet us on future trips and immediately take us to the Lady Luck casino for a late-night breakfast.

For going home, we were still in coach on the train, but thankfully now on the direct path to Chicago instead of the A to Z route. But it was still winter, with a blizzard blanketing the Midwest.

Our train adventure got a little screwy once we arrived in Iowa. It was night. The heavy snow was making the tracks impassible. Nothing on the train was working. No cafe. No food. Plus the water had frozen so the coach cars were down to one bathroom. Uh-oh. I was already looking outside for available spots.

A food truck finally pulled up to our train. Crates of sandwiches were unloaded and brought on board where people tried to lunge for the morsels like starving refugees. Luckily the porter was a master at crowd control. His goal was to make sure everyone on board got a free sandwich. Yes, free, which probably accounted for the rush of humanity.

"One sandwich per person. The one you touch is the one you take," was the porter's mantra repeated throughout the train and heard around the world that night as he handed out sandwiches.

The train got rolling again and we arrived in Chicago around 11 p.m. on New Year's Eve. People huddled outside the station in the blizzard looking for cabs. My dad, bless his heart, was determined to get us to a hotel that night. My word, an actual hotel. It also helped that the train company handed out vouchers for a free night's hotel stay. He hailed a cab like a veteran New Yorker and we all piled in, leaving the crowd behind.

'One Sandwich Per Person,' winter 1976-77

We got to the hotel and I was the last to get out of the cab. My dad paid the driver, and I, suffering from a lack of taxi etiquette, waited for the change. The cabbie gave it to me and I left, not giving the poor guy anything for a tip. I didn't know about tipping. He was even nice enough to return the small suitcase we left in the trunk of the cab to the hotel.

What a treat it was to sleep horizontally for a change. Another treat was hearing music all night up in our room from the band playing in the hotel lounge.

POSSIBLE TRANSPORTATION MODE!

TIME TO GO!

BURNED IN BILOXI

TRAIN LOVER, SAW THE BEATLES.

54

THE NEGOTIATOR!

MY NIECES: FREQUENT FLYERS!

THE HOME BASE

WEDDING CRASHERS

OFF TO THE CAPTAIN'S DINNER

MY DAD'S PRE-TRIP CHECKLISTS

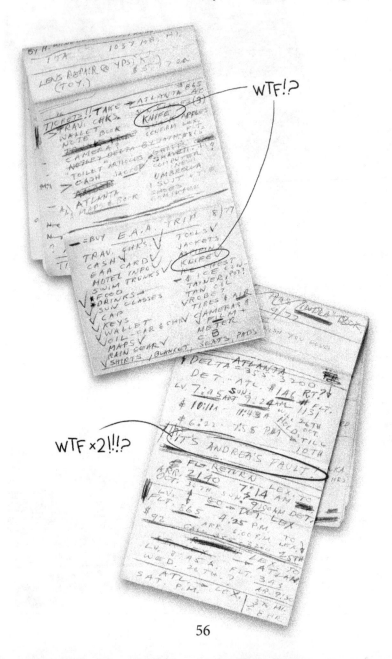

WTF!?

WTF x2!!!?

Chapter Eight

Connecticut or Bust:
The wedding, January 1982

You would have thought the blizzard of 1977 would have deterred us from traveling in the winter. But no.

It started innocently enough when I was preparing for final exams at my college in Texas. I received a telegram (!) at my dorm. I thought it was a warning from my parents about passing my tests or don't bother coming home. Instead it was from my brother announcing his wedding in Connecticut in January. I was thrilled, not for my brother, well, yeah a bit, but more selfishly for the fact my family and I would be visiting the New York area during the holidays. I figured the wedding would be a great entrée for taking side trips to the city.

I saw New York all right, but it was upstate New York,

not the city. Schenectady, Rochester, Buffalo, Binghampton; places we had traveled through in summer but now we were going through in the dead of winter. No train this time. Back in the car. Oh, dear. My parents, middle sister, non-Vegas brother and I embarked on this adventure at night. Why we left at night remains a mystery to this day.

My oldest sister wanted to also go with us, but after she saw that five people were going in our hatchback station wagon, she thought twice. Smart move on her part. She sized up the car and realized there wasn't enough room for her and stayed behind with her two young children. I felt bad for her that she wasn't going to experience this road trip. She wasn't. She actually preferred the train, a trait she passed on to her kids.

My dad was always prepared for a blizzard in Detroit. The trunk of his car was prepped like a tank going into battle: bags of salt, fox shovel, flares, flashlights, heat source of a candle in a coffee can, blankets, tools and Spacefood sticks. But for some reason these necessities never made it to our car for this trip. No room, either.

It wouldn't have been so bad leaving that night if the temperature had climbed above at least 30 degrees. It would have been even better if our trip wasn't planned at the last minute with us rushing around and forgetting blankets and heavy winter jackets. Food would have been nice, too.

We said farewell to our warm house and beds and proceeded out the driveway headed for Ontario and then New York state. My brother, sister and I were in the back seat and barely five minutes down the road when my sister jokingly stretched her legs across our laps and fell asleep. Who still traveled like this at our age? Oh, I know, our family did.

To get to Windsor, Ont., we had to get through Canadian Customs. I'm sure the agent wondered why would five adults packed into a car be leaving Michigan late at night? It was probably too cold for him to talk, and the next thing I remember we were driving along Lake Erie, pitch black and foreboding. Some things I've only seen at night. Lake Erie was one of them. It was only decades later that I finally saw it during the daytime on a flight to New York City. Gee, what a novelty.

Snow was starting to fall on the Ontario highway. My feet were getting cold in the back seat as I was only wearing a flimsy ski jacket. Worthless. I'd never be able to survive on those wilderness shows. This is when my limited knowledge of mechanical engineering kicked in. I figured if the outside temperature was bitter cold, then the car engine cooled off quicker, thus not producing substantial heat. We kept driving despite the cold. There were no exit ramps loaded with motel choices or all-night restaurants back then. Just an empty highway. Maybe that was why we traveled a lot at night.

First big stop: Buffalo and the New York State Thruway. We bypassed the entire Niagara Falls thing because, well, it was closed at that hour. It was maybe midnight. Most of the local gas stations were closed, too. We stopped somewhere so my dad could venture into the cramped back seat next to my mom and sister and sleep. No wonder he would always declare during many of these excursions: "When I get home, I'm going to take a real vacation."

Now my brother was at the wheel like a co-pilot of a troubled plane. I was up front, too, enjoying the leg room, instant heat and control of the radio. All was right except for the pangs of nausea and dizziness from seeing nothing but darkness outside. Kind of like that spatial disorientation. Thankfully we were on the ground.

We left Buffalo and were cruising on the thruway with no other cars around. Of course not, anyone else at that hour was home asleep. All we saw were flickering lights from inside homes tucked high on the hillsides. The wind was picking up, but inside the car we felt warm and safe. I don't know about the people in the back seat, but up front was toasty. My toes thawed.

So your job as second-in-command is to keep the first-in-command awake. My brother would always enjoy looking like he was asleep at the wheel whenever I'd glance his way. He must have picked up that trick from my dad. My other job was to find a decent radio station. At night in the Adirondack foothills?

The miles passed. Our eyes were now focused on the dwindling gas. With all the fuss getting through Buffalo, we forget to fill up the tank. Nothing for miles. No road signs announcing the nearest gas station. No 24-hour truckstops. No 24-hour anything. Did we dare risk life by waking up our dad and telling him our predicament? We decided no. That's all we needed was five people fighting over who forgot to get the gasoline.

We quietly debated about just pulling over onto the highway shoulder and calling it a night (hoping Big Foot wouldn't appear) when we saw a billboard claiming gas and food, open all night, next exit. We left the thruway and drove into this sleepy town near Ithaca,

N.Y., looking for any signs of life. Nothing.

Then we found the station but it was closed, with a "*Please come again!*" sign on its front door. I wanted to rig the gas pump anyway, but it was too cold to leave the car. Now we had no choice but to wake up the captain. That was fun.

Back on the thruway we went. We finally found a rest stop with a few trucks parked for the night. No cars. Just our car. The place was atop a mountain ridge with winds howling around the car and through the windows. I never heard of hypothermia but I'm sure we all experienced some as we struggled to stay warm in the car. And we still hadn't found gasoline. That would have to wait until morning, if we survived the night. Dun. Dun. Dun.

As soon as we parked the car, everyone lunged for position. My dad was back in the driver's seat with the extra legroom. I had the other front seat while my brother, mom and sister and were stuck in the back with the blanket. One blanket! But no leg room. I had plenty of leg room but nothing to keep me warm other than my ski jacket. I used my skimpy ski vest (I have never skied in my life) for a pillow until my father eyed it. He must have moved in for the kill after I had passed out from the cold because my vest was under his head the rest of the night.

I woke up the next morning with a foot by my face. The foot looked very cold. First order of business was buying gas to get going. The next need was food. This is when my mother resurfaced, making sure we got the best bang for our buck at the tight-fisted cafes that dotted the outskirts of the thruway. It was rare to get refills on coffee back then. My sister was too dizzy to care where we ate, but just wanted to eat like *now*. Good luck with that in our family. My mother's prowess for evaluating meals, menus and their monetary value was second to none. You just had to be patient. Eventually we found breakfast in some small, country store. I think we ate while standing.

Now we were back on the road, heading through the Catskills. We stopped briefly at the famous and historic Grossinger's Resort near Liberty, N.Y. My brother at the time worked in hotels. Somehow my mother, the negotiator, got him a makeshift meet-and-greet with an assistant manager of sorts at this resort. Nothing like spending the night in a coffee can only to wake up the next day and be sitting in an interview.

At last we rolled into Connecticut. Still cold. It was

very nice to get to the hotel, but no time to sit and re-lax. I was off to the city! My groom-to-be brother and his bride-to-be and I left to pick up one of his friends flying into JFK and then onto dinner. You know, look-ing back, it probably would have been a good idea for me to have showered but that never figured in as I was exhausted from the trip and not thinking clearly.

After dinner at a nice Italian place in Valley Stream on Long Island, I picked up clues that I might be a lit-tle rank when my brother's friend kept commenting on a rather odd odor inside the car. I just played stu-pid. Luckily the topic changed, literally, when we ap-proached a toll bridge for Connecticut and my brother tossed coins at the toll kiosk's wide basket but missed it by a mile. Coins went everywhere. Geesus. Now we had every car in New York City honking at us to get the hell out of the way as my poor brother scrambled to pick up the loose change. But he was used to stressful situa-tions, having fended off the dog at the B&B in Maine.

The wedding and reception were all splendid. Unfor-tunately there was no time for us to see the big city. And frankly, I couldn't really picture my dad driving around in New York. I have no recollection of the trip home to Detroit. Probably just as well. Why would it be any dif-ferent than the outbound odyssey?

Chapter Nine

Wishing You Were Here

Crisscrossed: Apparently when I was very, very little or maybe not even born, my folks and the rest of our gang were driving to Milwaukee, where my mom and dad were from, to see my mom's parents. At the same time, her parents were driving to Detroit to see us. We must have all been traveling on a small highway. And I guess communication at the time was uncalled for as my mom thought she saw her dad's car, with her dad and stepmother in it, pass us by. Sure enough. We arrived in Milwaukee; they made it to Detroit. Nobody was home at either place. "Boy, were they mad," my mom recalled.

The high seas: Growing up I was reminded that when I was 2 years old I developed some "rash" and was not allowed to board some ship. Maybe that's when my fears of abandonment during our travels started. Years later my oldest sister told me the cruise folks thought I had the measles. But my mother, the nurse, had convinced them it was heat rash. I was eventually let onboard and thankfully have no memory of the confrontation. I thought this trip was to South America since we were on the S.S. *South American*. Think again. My sister said it was a ship that sailed the Great Lakes, including Detroit to Buffalo and back. Buffalo!! But she said that our family "for once had a room on the top deck instead of the bottom deck" and aside from me being a health hazard, it was a rather pleasant trip.

Another family vacation was taking a cruise from Florida to Nassau in the Bahamas in the early 1960s. My oldest sister recalled all of us piled into a car and driving south on the smaller U.S. highways before some of the interstates were completed in this area. We got lost in northern Georgia but my dad still drove the rest of the night to Florida, where my sister said we slept in our car in a hospital parking lot. I see a trend here. The other highlight was her, at maybe age 14, buying miniature liquor bottles for my parents at a store in Nassau. No identification necessary!

Going batty: I should be used to bats. I think this

started when I was a toddler of sorts and our family was staying in Vermont in a hotel. My mom said everyone was asleep when there was suddenly something flying around the room. A bat. Thankfully I remember none of this.

The bat incidents I do remember occurred much later in life when visiting my sister's nice house in southern Indiana. Smaller towns seem to have more wooded areas, which to me translates to more bats. Two different visits, two different bats. Always in the room where I chose to slept. At night I listened for any rustling and then sure enough, I would see wings flying at me, skirting my head. I hid in bed and used my cell phone to call my sister -- I had her number on speed dial -- upstairs so she could wake up her husband, the outdoorsman, to catch the bats. He's two for two!

Seeing stars: This trip was to Toronto in maybe 1964 or 1965. What I would have given for digital cameras back then, even if I was only 3 years old. Apparently my family was in town for some Canadian expo. My oldest sister again recalls all of us staying at a pretty decent hotel. "Two rooms for once," she said. "Amazing," she added. But then, the manager moved our family off that top floor because the Beatles were in town and staying at the hotel, thus needing the entire floor.

Like, *whatever.* Later my mom hurried my oldest sister and brother to the crowded lobby where they actually saw the Beatles at a distance being rushed into a private elevator. My poor brother was even pushed and his glasses were knocked off in the mayhem, but he was scrappy and played hockey, so I'm sure he was ready to drop his winter gloves to start a scuffle.

Thanksgiving travel: We took a lot of mini-road trips during the Thanksgiving break. Once to Washington, D.C., where my parents were married. This was all planned in 1963, and coincided a week after the president's assassination. My family toured the White House, with its windows and fireplace mantels still draped in black mourning crepe.

We also went to Kentucky several times for the holiday. We had a great turkey dinner at Ft. Knox and we weren't even military. Our family stayed at a hotel where Jesse James lived (doesn't everyone hear that in Kentucky?) and we visited Mammoth Cave (hey, more bats). The caves were very cool and lots of fun, especially walking over the wobbly "bottomless pit" bridge with your pushy brother behind you.

Chapter Ten

Yet Another East Coast Trip, summer 1992-ish?

My mom was tracking her genealogy and needed to do research in Connecticut. She, my dad and I planned another road trip. This time we left in daylight! I think we made it to middle Pennsylvania on the first day. Beautiful countryside there. But once again we had the problem of being stuck in a rural area with limited motel choices.

We found a small motor lodge up on a hill with a driveway the size of an overhead luggage bin where maybe six cars could squeeze in side-by-side. The manager's office was like a prison guard tower, with full view of every room door and occupants coming and going. There were probably about 10 rooms with a maximum of two people per room or it would cost extra.

Here we go. I was the extra. As we drove into the parking lot, I immediately took cover in the back seat of our small two-door. But I was determined not to sleep scrunched up in our car in the middle of nowhere just to hear a tapping sound on the window at night by who-knows-what just to save some bucks. I offered to pay my parents, I think the extra $45, but my mom had a better idea. "We'll just sneak you in and out." Great. I'm nearly six feet tall. My dad, however, volunteered to do the sneaking. He thought it would be fun.

Somehow it worked. Nobody broke into the room at night demanding payment because we know that extra $45 went to buy the powdered doughnuts and powdered orange juice that were offered as the 'breakfast" portion of the morning's advertised meal. And please, only take ONE doughnut. The manager watched my mom and me like a hawk when we entered the office, which also doubled as the breakfast nook. How the hell was I going to sneak an extra doughnut PLUS coffee with two creams and one sugar to my dad? The dilemma. I think my mom deployed a distraction technique, and suddenly I was out the door, mission complete.

We escaped the hotel and proceeded east to New York City. But this time we were heading north of the city into New Haven, Conn.

Yet Another East Coast Trip, summer 1992-ish?

We found a great hotel, where all the extras were allowed to stay for free, along the Long Island Sound. My mom got her research done. I was feeling very content to hang out there a few days near the 1-95 corridor when my dad announced, "OK, let's go home." Go where? We just got here? Well, at least we left for home in the daylight.

My mom had more family research to do near Westerlo, N.Y., in the Hudson Valley. The drive was beautiful through the wooded areas along the Hudson River. We spent the night at a real hotel in Kingston. But what had been a beautiful summer day's drive was suddenly turning eerily dark with stormy, green skies. Rumbles of thunder could be heard in the distance. My parents - both unafraid of storms - were having dinner somewhere. I have no idea why I wasn't eating with them. And I had no idea where they went.

I have always had a huge fear of storms and now I was alone in this room, top floor naturally, with this severe storm approaching. The storm warnings on the television kept flashing like a 100 counties that were in the line of fire. I had no idea what county we were in. Since this was pre-internet, I searched the phone book hoping I would discover the name of the county so I could take immediate cover in the bathroom. Thinking back,

I could have just called the front desk.

I've always been stuck in some motel room with a ferocious thunderstorm approaching. Denton, Texas. Biloxi, Miss. Bentonville, Ark. Memphis. Manchester, Tenn., (I had to wake up my mom for that and we both ended up in the closet - she's such a trooper). The pattern here is Southern cities. How naive of me to think storms didn't happen in upstate New York.

Thankfully the motel survived and the next day we headed home. *That was one quick trip east.* We took a different route through lower New York state, which I'd never seen. Very pretty but hilly with winding roads and lots and lots of driving all done by yours truly. I didn't mind. It seemed like 18 months had passed before we finally exited New York State. Of course, the last stretch of Interstate 86 near Jamestown, N.Y., was only two lanes of facing traffic for endless miles because of construction. At night, naturally. One wrong move and forget about it. I had a kung fu grip on the steering wheel and my eyes were like lasers scanning the road. No distractions, just drive. Thankfully my parents' commentary was held to a minimum.

We finally made it to the Ohio Turnpike where once again I'm seeing Lake Erie at night. I was exhausted and my eyes were burning. Beats me why there was no hotel room waiting for me after that yeoman's job of driving, but I convinced myself that sitting upright in the driver's seat at this truck stop we pulled into at the last minute was just the same.

And of course, my dad, the eager beaver who slept like a rock in the back seat, couldn't wait to get going the next morning back to Detroit. I said, "Fine. Here, you drive," and handed him the keys.

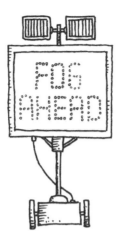

Chapter Eleven

Here and There

Texas and Matamoros, Mexico: winter, mid-1970s

I have had the good fortune of visiting five Tex-Mex border cities, two for just five minutes. Brownsville, Texas, and Matamoros, Mexico. This time I didn't even have a chance to leave our car and drink the water.

I don't know why my dad, mom, two of my brothers and I (us three in our teens) decided to travel by train to Mexico City during this Christmas break. I remember my middle brother packing his fancy sunglasses and travel money. I'm like, you ain't going to Vegas here. But the way we traveled, Las Vegas could have easily ended up on our itinerary.

This trip fell apart at the last minute. At some point, one would have hoped my parents had just moved to Texas giving us quicker access to our beloved Mexico. The next thing I knew we piled into our station wagon (why not) in the dead of winter (but of course) to drive south. Instead of Mexico City, we aimed for some place closer along the Mexican border.

Let's do the math. We had three drivers and it was about 1,660 miles or a 3 day from Detroit to Matamoros. The average driving day was 8 to 9 hours. We had maybe 1 week to get there and back. That was 3 days down and 3 days back, leaving us 1 day to actually do something outside the car.

I have no idea where we stayed between here and there, or why we would think Mexico City and Matamoros were interchangeable as travel destinations. I do remember, however, one of my brothers eating something bad at some burger joint near Waco, Texas, and while later touring the L.B.J. Library in Austin, he had an episode similar to my Nuevo Laredo water episode. Poor thing. Luckily I was spared any of that. I must have had the fish.

We arrived in Brownsville. It was neat to see the *very end* of an interstate. After going through Mexican customs with nothing to declare but our foolishness for taking this last-minute trip, we crossed the Rio Grande into Matamoros, albeit for about five minutes, because the driving was just too crazy for my dad, already exhausted from the mega-drive down. I think we saw some of the town, but I can't remember. There was no chance to take a picture.

Back in Texas we drove along the Gulf Coast for a few hours until we came to the realization that we didn't know what we were doing. We knew Texas was a very big state for driving, and we knew it was New Year's Eve. So what does a family of five sandwiched inside a station wagon with no hotel reservations do for fun? The parking lot across from the Johnson Space Center near Houston comes to mind. And that's where we spent New Year's Eve. I think we were hoping to visit the Space Center the next day, but with the holiday, no such luck. Oh well, it looked pretty cool at night. I'm still surprised we weren't arrested.

Biloxi, Miss.: spring and summer, late 1970s

Great coastal area with great beaches and lots of sun. Boy, what I'd given to have sunblock 278 for one of these trips. My mom, dad, brother and I would visit here, usually on spring break, from our home in Kentucky where my mom was now teaching. Once in Biloxi we stayed at nice, affordable hotels overlooking the water. I just wish we could have moved one these hotels to Meridian, Miss., because it seemed that was always the stopping point for our day's drive from the Bluegrass State. We stayed at a hospital parking lot in Meridian every time. It was also where I first ate grits – in the hospital cafeteria.

Denton, Texas: summer, mid-1970s

Now I remember why we spent a night or two in Des Moines, Iowa. We were on our way to Denton, Texas, where my mother was going to attend a nursing workshop. I recall the Des Moines event very well because we were eating dinner at some lonely restaurant along the interstate when a ferocious thunderstorm hit. We stayed there for shelter, then eventually returned to our motel where yet another storm blew in. And we weren't even in Texas yet.

My dad, mom, brother and I were on this trip. We traveled through St. Louis where we toured the arch. Then onto Denton, where oddly enough I'd find myself attending college there years later. I have no recall of the trip home to Detroit, but as these trips went, it was probably just as well.

Here and There

Eastern Kentucky: fall 1978

My mother was invited to a nursing conference in Atlanta and wanted my middle sister and me to come along. We would stay in a downtown hotel and check out the city. Sounded like a real vacation, plus I had never been to Atlanta.

But now my mom was worried about getting to Atlanta before 3 p.m. and didn't know what to expect along the road since we had never driven there. Estimated length of travel: 6 hours. Estimated time of departure from our Richmond, Ky., home: 4:30 a.m.

I didn't mind the early wake-up call, but my sister wasn't so thrilled. The back seat of the car became a continuation of her bed, and I, too young to drive, had to help my mom navigate up front. At 4:30 a.m. The only things on Interstate 75 at that hour were pickup trucks, big trucks and oversized trucks. And us.

Our driving arrangement lasted for about 30 minutes when we suddenly saw a huge road sign with its yellow lights flashing 'FOG AHEAD. USE CAUTION.' My mom and I thought it was the end of days. Sheer panic flooded our eyes. Fog banks appeared everywhere with trucks disappearing into them. The ups and downs and curves of the winding interstate made it even more exciting. My mom, bless her heart, wasn't a top-notch driver like these truckers, so I immediately begged my sister, who was a top-notch driver, to wake up and take control of the car like it was a plane going down. (She would later teach me a lot about driving, like how to manage the expressway through northern Kentucky, at the time known as "Death Hill.")

But not this morning. My sister calmly suggested we find a rest stop and wait until daylight when she would take over driving. We found a truck stop of sorts and parked in a rear, gravel lot. I was in the driver's seat, nodding off, when suddenly a truck with a trailer bed full of lumber was backing up in front of our car. I beeped the car horn before the two-by-fours crashed into the windshield. The truck stopped, the boards inches from the glass. Thankfully the trucker didn't come back yelling at us, but I'm sure he wondered why three women were sleeping in a car in the back of a truck stop.

I think that was the last time we ever left our Kentucky home that early for any road trip.

Ice roads: Kentucky-Ohio-Michigan, winter 1982

My brother and his newlywed wife decided on a rustic honeymoon in central Kentucky. It was winter and a pretty time of year in the state. After their vacation they were planning to drive to Detroit. With me along, of course.

I'm not sure if it was a smart idea to drive. This Kentucky to Detroit trip usually took 8 hours in good weather. Now there was a looming blizzard with bitter, dangerous cold. Ah, yes, leave it to us to test Mother Nature in a Nova (my favorite family car). Chances were, too, it would get even colder as we drove from south to north. And it did!

The first bad sign was seeing nobody traveling that day. Not even trucks. The second bad sign was my feet were already cold and we hadn't even gotten to Cincinnati. I'm surprised the car windows didn't crack. I sat in the back seat wearing once again a flimsy ski jacket. I exercised my feet to stay warm. The front seats resembled the Rocky Mountains, blocking any hot air. The third bad sign was our car was low on gas and we didn't see any open gas stations. Signs read, "*Closed. Too cold to pump the gas.*" Thanks. At least the interstate was still visible until we hit central Ohio. Good thing nobody was on the road because all that blowing snow mixed with extra cars could have posed a problem.

Tagging along: Washington, D.C., August mid-1970s

Here I am again, crashing the party. This time, for some reason, I really, really wanted to go with my parents on their trip to Washington, D.C., to celebrate their anniversary. I think I was a last minute add-on, like sunflower seeds to a salad, because my parents were practically down our driveway in their car when they stopped and let me tag along.

Another road trip east. And I couldn't even help my dad drive. We made it to Washington in one piece and enjoyed watching from the car the endless construction of the district's future underground transportation. Road construction is always fun in the summer. (My favorite had to be Nashville's 10-year highway improvement project.) At least we stayed in a comfortable hotel for this trip, but as always something was kind of screwy here. This was a massive hotel, with multiple wings and maybe 10 floors to each wing. Luckily for us, we practically had an entire wing to ourselves. But wait, every room and floor looked dark and empty. Did we not get the memo? I never left our room alone.

A port in the storm: Lima, Ohio, fall 1986

While living in Ohio, I convinced a friend to travel

with me by train and plane to see my brother and his wife in Georgia. Simple enough. Fly there. Train back through D.C., then back home to Ohio. We arrived in Atlanta without a problem. My brother worked at a large downtown hotel, where the staff was handing out free tickets, kind of like you did for a county fair, to hear then-President Reagan speak at the hotel. So that was neat despite having to wait hours in the sun with hundreds of our closest friends to get into the convention hall to hear the president's speech.

Another day my friend and I took a city bus or train up to Midtown Atlanta to browse the shops, museums and cafes. You know, I must really work harder at measuring traveling distances by foot. I suggested we just walk back to the hotel. O.K. I thought it would be *fun*. What started as a pleasant walk with sun turned into a marathon of sorts trudging through streets as we braced for the cold winds heading back to our hotel, where, exhausted, we downed pots of the best room service coffee (courtesy of my big bro) just to warm up.

Then a few days later, it was back to Ohio. Some people can sleep on trains. Others can't. Oh, well. It wasn't that long of a train trip by my standards. Two days and two nights. Too bad I didn't read that itinerary better because had I known we'd arrive in Lima, our stopping point, at around 5 a.m. .... Before we left, my sister, also living in Ohio, had graciously offered to pick us up in Lima, about two hours from her home. Funny how that slips one's mind when you get that 5 a.m. phone call on a chilly, fall morning. Sure, we can wait a few hours. We'll just sit here in the station and look at each other.

That was wishful thinking because no sooner had the train left and any offloading passengers had been picked up, the station closed. Now what does one do at this hour in Lima standing outside the station with luggage and no cell phones? I suggested we walk somewhere. That's when my friend's eyes glazed over. More walking? At this hour? The one road next to the station led past warehouses and some rickety shacks, while the other road - wait, that was the only road. The other exit route was the train tracks. We didn't really walk on the tracks, but instead parallel, hoping to avoid oncoming freight trains. We thought downtown might be ahead but I couldn't see right as my eyes were so blurry from a lack of sleep.

We saw lights and a street with actual businesses after about a 15 minute walk facing a brisk, northerly wind - I'm still astonished we didn't get mugged. We were pretty sure we were still in Lima, however there was no one around to ask. The stores weren't open yet, but wait, a bar was. Who knew at this hour? But this wasn't any bar, this was heaven-sent.

We stepped inside the wood-paneled tavern and immediately felt warmth from a roaring fire in the fireplace. The lighting was soft, perfect for my migraine. And we were just in time for breakfast. We ate like two sailors on leave, then afterward dozed in our cozy booth. Pure luxury stumbled upon by mistake. The best kind. I'm glad it was midweek so nobody tossed us out, either, after our eighth cup of coffee as we waited for daylight and my sister. I didn't want to tell her to retrieve us at this bar, not that she would care, so we wandered back to the station, this time on a real road as it was daylight.

That was the most exercise I ever had on a train trip.

Chapter Twelve

Flights to Remember

One time flying from Columbus to Washington, D.C. (this time without my parents), there were about a dozen folks onboard this 757. Those were the days. Before takeoff, we were all instructed to move to first class, leaving coach entirely empty. Then we were served champagne and hot towels. Some flights you never want to end.

Other flights you do. Like an evening flight I took once from Atlanta to California. Kind of stormy out, so the captain kept the seat-belt sign on from Atlanta to Lawton, Okla. No big deal, but it was dinnertime and us passengers had not received their free drink or bag of pretzels. And you know what that means. No sooner than the seat-belt sign turned off, passengers bolted from their seats for either the bathrooms or to get drinks. The cabin suddenly looked like the floor of a stock exchange. Flight attendants scrambled for position and served up beverages faster than a Vegas bartender looking for tips.

London: spring 1993

This was a quick trip. So quick in fact I flew with a co-worker to London for the weekend. From Los Angeles. It was a bargain of a plane fare. We left Thursday night and came back Monday afternoon. Back at work on Tuesday.

Columbus to Los Angeles: January 1988

Then there was my flight for a job interview in California. My first clue something could be amiss was at the airport ticket counter in Columbus, where I lived. The airline agent told me my ticket would cost about $562. Come again? My perspective employer forgot to pay for the ticket. Sigh. Maybe that was a good thing since a massive winter storm was slamming Southern California that same day, or it could have been a sign of things to come ...

We decided to retry this affair the next weekend. All

worked out. My future employer dropped some Benjamins for the ticket and now I was flying west with a connection in Denver. I'm minding my own business near the front of the plane when I hear a gentleman in the back of the plane shout, "Fire!" "She's on fire!"

Now I'm thinking, do I really want to turn around and see all this? And did he say, "she?" Did this woman self-combust?

Alas, I turned around just in time to see this guy whip off his shirt and start smacking a headrest with it. While he was trying to be all macho, a female flight attendant calmly moved his ass out of the way and grabbed a fire extinguisher to douse the smoldering seat cover. Done. Over. Now put your shirt back on, please.

A woman with styling gel in her hair had fallen asleep, cigarette in hand, and her hair caught on fire, thus the headrest burning, thus the guy yelling "FIRE" in a packed airplane at 35,000 feet. I thought, O.K., if we're going down, I'm going to listen to some good music. We landed safely in Denver where paramedics boarded the plane and helped the poor woman out, her burned head now bandaged.

On to Cali. Finally arrived late at night, hoping my sister and my infant niece were already at the nearby hotel. I had brought a special birthday cake for my sister from her favorite bakery in Columbus. I was holding the cake box as I exited the plane down an old-fashioned ramp, marveling at how the cake survived the "fire" and the Denver connection only to watch the box fall helplessly out of my hands and tumble onto the tarmac. We still ate it.

My sister was trying to be incognito at this hotel, since my perspective employer was only paying for me and not my entire family. Too bad my mom and I weren't aware of her plan as we both called the hotel to alert them of my flight schedule and my sister's arrival. Sure enough, when my sister entered the hotel trying to go unnoticed, a clerk called out to her, "Your mother just called and your sister is on her way."

The flight home to Ohio was fine, other than it being the last plane to land during an approaching blizzard.

Last one leaving: early 1990s

I must have wanted airline miles badly because I took the last flight at night from L.A. to San Francisco. Then from San Francisco, I took the red-eye and last flight of the night to Washington, D.C. It was like I was the last one in the airport, so please turn off the lights. It was also summer. Midway through the flight I kept seeing flashing lights outside my window. I was half awake until I realized it was lightning and it was getting closer. Now I was wide awake. I closed the window shade when I saw the plane's landing lights come on so the pilots could see the storm clouds ahead. That was enough for me. Luckily we avoided the storms. This was the first flight where I lost a piece of luggage. I think it finally arrived by courier days later at my brother's house at 2 a.m.

The only other time I lost luggage, also in Washington, D.C., was during a presidential inauguration weekend. I arrived at the airport "luggage desk" to fill out forms. I could have stayed there for hours, not because of delays, but rather for the delicious coffee service that was available to the "distressed" passengers. I had never seen so many free coffee and tea samples, flavored creamers and real cream, plus a wild assortment of cookies and snacks. Phenomenal.

Los Angeles airport: various years

Just like visiting many Tex-Mex border towns, I've also been fortunate to stay at nearly every hotel around the Los Angeles airport region even when I lived not far away. Now I know what that sounds like, but these stays were all travel or family related. One of my favorite hotels faced several small houses, complete with fenced-in roosters that were better than any alarm clock.

One night I slept outside an airline's terminal gates - not the ones leading to the planes - but the actual metal gates that came down from the ceiling and locked into place in the floor. I was dropped off by a friend catching a red-eye and I thought I could just crash, sorry, just sleep somewhere in the terminal until my flight the next morning. I was wrong. I ended up sleeping outside the gates on the cold, tiled floor. I was soon joined by some Aussies. By morning there was a crowd of at least seven travelers.

I'm like a dog. I can sleep on any surface. But dogs aren't bothered by panhandlers at 4 a.m. looking for money. This guy was kicking my shoes and wanting change for the bus. THE BUS?? Was I dreaming about a previous trip?

Bear hunting: Prince George, B.C., summer 1998

One of my sisters and her family were now living in northern British Columbia. I was down in Southern California. The quickest way to get to their house was to fly. I was hoping for a nonstop flight from LAX to

Prince George. On a big jet. Well, half of the flight was that way to Seattle. Then I thought they were joking when my next flight to Vancouver was on a very small prop job. I'm like, what happened here people? Not that I was afraid, but when you're thinking twin engines and you see twin props it just gives you a pause. I got an even bigger pause after landing safely in Vancouver and found my way to the Prince George gate. There I saw folks walking outside. Once again, I had to walk the tarmac to another prop job. This one sat maybe 20 passengers and I think had a big moose painted on the fuselage.

Now I was on the afternoon, two-hour flight headed north over snowy, mountainous terrain on a plane that buzzed and lurched every time we hit a crosswind. I kept thinking we were going to end up in a movie of the week. The mostly male passengers were yakkers and I was quite proud of the young, female flight attendant when she told them to shut up while she was instructing us on the plane's safety features. Yes, people, shut up, *I want to hear all of this.* They were rattling on about bear hunting and their bear guns. That was a topic of conversation I hadn't heard before while flying.

As an aside, you don't ever want to say "gum" while flying. I had placed my chewing gum in a bag in the overhead aboard a cross-country flight and needed it before landing. I reached up and sifted through my carry-on, with one nice gentleman asking me if I needed help. I said, "No, thanks. I'm just looking for my gum." See, with the loud engines droning, I thought, uh-oh, that didn't sound right. Then someone else offered to get out of my way, and again, I said, "I'm just looking for my gum." After that, I was quick to remember to say "chewing gum" and keep some on my person.

We landed safely in Prince George, but I was still kind of traumatized by the entire event. As soon as I arrived at my sister's house, I hugged my two nieces who were so happy to see me yet dismayed when I practically knocked them over looking for the phone so I could call the airline and train people (just like my mom) to find an alternate way home. There was no time for my young nieces to discuss aircraft with me. We loved to go to the airport and watch planes, and I remember fondly when one of them asked me, "Is a 757 bigger than a 737?" I trained them well.

Now I was hoping for a 737 for the trip home. No luck. I kept my reservations and was quite happy to see the BAE-146 four engine jet at the Prince George airport awaiting my departure. Back in Vancouver, my fear had subsided and I handled the prop plane to Seattle like a pro. Otherwise I'd still be up in Prince George with the bear hunters.

Birthday wishes: summer, early 1990s

I'm usually good at predicting when weather will affect my flights, like if it's going to storm and cause delays, it will the minute the flight attendants lock and cross-check the cabin doors. That's what happened on a flight from Atlanta to Detroit to L.A. (Hey, sounds like a train trip.) On my birthday. The deluge caused delays that rippled across my itinerary.

I had no time to visit my parents that day when I changed planes in Detroit, but I did call them. Nothing more melancholy than calling someone when you land at their airport but not being able to leave to see them.

Then it was off to Los Angeles. But now because of the delays, I wasn't arriving at a respectable 9 p.m; instead it was pushing midnight when we landed. Exhausted from the flight, I hailed a shuttle bus for the remote parking lot and settled in for the short ride, but one that given the shuttle drivers in L.A., could still bring harm. Onboard the shuttle I chatted with a young couple and their son, who looked about 12. They had vacationed in Hawaii for his birthday, which turned out to be that day, the same as mine.

Luckily I met these folks and luckily they had parked their car near mine, because the first thing I saw on my car was a flat tire. The dad graciously helped me change the tire. Well, he changed the tire. I just gathered up the 293 newspapers sitting in my station wagon hatchback, above the spare tire compartment, making a mental note to keep a cleaner car.

Now it was about 1 a.m. and I had a doughnut on my car. I wasn't smart enough yet to belong to an auto club. So I decided to get a hotel room near the Los Angeles airport and drive home the next day with my doughnut at 45 mph. My parents were still waiting on my phone call to let them know I made it home, but with no cell phones then, they had to wait.

Finally checked in at an airport hotel, I took my key and practically slept in the elevator to my floor. Then I opened my room door, anticipating a bed, but instead was greeted by a chain and dead bolt. And someone yelling at me: "You've got the wrong room." I wasn't going to argue. Not at that hour.

I trudged back down to the front desk and got yet another key. I had no idea what time it was, or really where I was, but once safely in my room, I called my parents. They just asked if I had had a good trip! They were also quite relieved that I didn't drive home on the 405 at 1 a.m. doing 45 mph.

Earthquake! June 1992

I learned the hard way about not telling my parents or family of any weekend travel. Like when I flew from Los Angeles to San Francisco to visit my Ohio co-worker (still talking to me after the Lima train incident) who now lived in the Bay Area. This was the weekend a major earthquake hit the L.A. desert. Of course I wasn't watching the news and we had no cell phones and nobody knew where I was. My family couldn't reach me. That went over well. I just went for the *weekend*. I included my folks in the loop after that, mainly so I didn't have to hear about it any more. ...

Bankruptcy blues: DFW Airport, May 1982

You want to see stadium-sized crowds at an airport? Be there EXACTLY when an airline files for bankruptcy and grounds all its flights. That's what I witnessed at DFW around midday on a flight home to Detroit. Braniff Airlines was based in Dallas and thankfully I was flying Texas International. I should have sold my ticket to the highest bidder.

Security, please

I always enjoy traveling with my mother. Never a dull moment. I remember taking her on a 1996 flight from Detroit to Los Angeles to stay with me for awhile. She hadn't flown since the early 1980s, and that was when she flew home from Ceylon. I'm thinking, this is just a five hour flight, not 24 hours. She can handle it! But she was understandably nervous. I was, too, not knowing what could happen with her at higher altitudes, and heaven help us, we also had to change planes in Chicago, and it was raining.

The night before the flight, my mom was in her bedroom and I was in mine, but that didn't stop her from talking aloud to me through the walls about the pros and cons of flying west, what to expect, do we get meals, etc. I could tell she was nervous just by her rambling. At one point, I said: "There's turbulence, you know." She replied, "I know." Made me long for the bus. But our fears were for naught as both plane rides were fine, thus once again opening more travel doors for my mom.

After that experience, my mom flew with me on several trips. I always had to prep her, however, for security, like what to wear, how to pack. Silly me, leaving her carry-on bags unattended at home for an upcoming vacation. The next day at the airport, one of the security agents took my mom and her carry-on aside for inspection. (This was pre-9/11.) Now what? It's just clothes, I thought. Then my mom whispered to me, "I wonder if he's looking at that knife?" KNIFE!? My mom had innocently put a large steak knife -- and some fruit -- into her bag, all to be used during the flight for a snack. We made it onto the plane, and so did the fruit, but the knife didn't.

The best part of traveling with my mom was whenever she would go through the metal detector screening machines. Most folks do exactly as they are told, with their arms either down by their sides or up over their heads. Whenever my mom used a wheelchair, she would quickly hop out of that chair and enter the screening machine, snapping to attention as she made a quick Michael Jackson dance move with great flourish. Then she would just freeze, looking like a mannequin.

Fill 'er up!

I finally figured out after maybe 20 years of renting cars while on "vacation," usually seeing my dear family, it was best to prepay for the gasoline. I can't count the number of times the gas didn't fill up all the way, forcing me to try it again. Or the gas pump didn't work in the bitter cold. Or it was 5 a.m. in the country and no gas stations were open. Then what? But my two favorite episodes for pumping gas were while returning rental cars in Detroit and Atlanta.

At this gas station near the Detroit airport, I clicked on the pump's auto shut-off valve on the handle, and like a fool, stepped away to check on something, thinking the pump would shut off when the tank was full. The tank was full of gasoline all right and so was the side of the car and tire below and the ground. I rushed to put the pump back, spilling gas on my shoes, but luckily not my pants. That would come later.

Now here I was literaly fuming, moments before entering the airport and reeking of gasoline. Thankfully, and I don't know why because my feet are so large that an extra pair of shoes takes up valuable luggage space, I *did* have an extra pair of shoes in my luggage. I found an out-of-the way bathroom, still choking on the gas fumes, and rinsed off everything. I couldn't wash my hands enough, highly afraid airport security might swipe them with that powder to reveal traces of explosive materials. I'm not sure what folks thought when they entered the bathroom and saw me washing my shoes in the sink. The shoes still smelled. I dumped them into the trash, and made it through security.

You'd think I had learned a lesson. Years later after visiting family again in Georgia, my friend and I were on the way to the airport and needed gas for the rental car. We found a station to fill up. Now this looked like a real pump with a real shut-off valve. But I crammed the pump too hard into the gas nozzle, ignoring the advice of my friend. Of course, she was right. I stepped away like an idiot, only to return to see what looked like Niagara Falls coming out of the gas tank. I lunged for the pump to stop the flow, but not before gasoline had doused my pants, but not my shoes (go figure). Once again I reeked of 87 unleaded, not to mention being upset that $10 worth of gas had spilled on the ground.

We had to think fast about my pants. The airport dogs might question the odor. I didn't have an extra pair in my luggage so we looked for any store that might have pants, but only found grocery stores and drugstores. I'm so glad at this time I didn't realize we only had about 90 minutes to get through airport security and to our gate. I thought we had at least three hours, but my numbers were a bit off. My family knows I like the extra hours at the airport, one time having spent at least six hours waiting for my flight at the Lexington, Ky., airport, which at the time only had about two gates.

By now I was nauseated from the fumes when suddenly we saw an outlet mall off the busy Atlanta highway. I made a hard, fast left turn like I was driving at Indy. We rushed inside the mall only to discover the oddest assortment of stores: jewelry, makeup, corn dogs, hats, and then, like an oasis, a clothing store. But it was men's big and tall of sorts, with rapper and military cargo pants.

I didn't care if I had to buy pants that made me look like a paratrooper boarding the plane. I just wanted breathing room from these noxious fumes. We found some blue jeans, nevermind they were one or two sizes too big. At least I wasn't tripping over them. This was probably the fastest sale the store clerk ever made. He could even smell me. I changed right there, well, in the dressing room, dumped my old pants and we made it to the airport with about 45 minutes to spare. Not just any airport, but the world's busiest, of course.

Chapter Thirteen

Graduation, summer 1983

The one benefit of not finding a job immediately after graduating college is the ability to travel. I highly recommend postponing a lifetime of work for a few months of leisure. It helped, too, that it was 1983 and one of the worst job markets ever. So I was able to enjoy months and months and months of leisure.

The only trip taken during this time was out west to visit my brothers in Las Vegas and San Francisco, and to attend my sister's graduation in Oregon. I picked the wrong year to graduate as it was also the same year my dad retired from a lifetime of work at a major car company, and my sister earned her Ph.D, just like my mom. So I was third in line on the excitement scale.

This time my mom and I took the train. From Detroit to Chicago to Los Angeles to Las Vegas back to Los Angeles up to San Francisco via Oakland, then on to Eugene, Ore., Seattle, Bellingham, Wash., and back to Portland. In coach. The route home was equally impressive in length.

Pretty uneventful trip through the Southwest until we arrived in La Junta, Colo. This is where my mom became a bit adventurous. But this woman, who was fortunate to travel around the world, was used to unexpected adventure. Like when she was alone and lost in Istanbul, Turkey, only to be assisted late in the day by a couple visiting from Michigan. What were the odds?

So she survives Istanbul but La Junta almost does her in. We were allowed maybe a half hour off the train to browse the quiet storefronts, including I think some discount bakery. Uh-oh. Twenty minutes had passed and my mom had disappeared. The next thing I remember I'm pleading with a conductor to hold the train. Like that always works.

I told the conductor my mom wasn't on the train yet, and could we wait for her, please? He of course said she better hurry. Minutes passed. Still no sign of my mother. Then I heard the dreaded words, "All aboard." I pleaded again with the conductor. His reply was simply, "Well, if you don't like it, you can wait here, too."

My mom finally appeared, holding a bakery bag. She was frantic. The train hadn't moved an inch, or that could have been an ugly sight, the two of us trying to hop a moving train. We returned to our seats, exhausted from the ordeal, when a sweet, elderly woman in the row ahead of us gave my mother a drink from her stash. Two tiny paper cups later, my mom was all relaxed.

Now it was on to Los Angeles where we would have the entire day to hang out before boarding the night train to Las Vegas.

Usually when people can spend a day in L.A. they visit the touristy places. We didn't. For some reason we decided to visit my brother's friend, who we met briefly before, in Beverly Hills. I knew this was a bad idea. If we could barely board the train in time in La Junta, how were we going to make it to the west side of L.A. and back? By bus, of course.

There we were, heading into the heart of the city with no maps, no watch and of course no cell phones. It was also a tad hot. Oven hot. No air conditioning on the bus. After a couple of missed directions and connec-

117

tions we arrived in Beverly Hills looking like we just walked through the desert. Hot, dusty, thirsty and our clothes drenched in sweat.

I don't know what possessed us to do this next, but we did it anyway. There in the ladies restroom of a posh Beverly Hills hotel, we took off our shirts and rinsed them in the sinks to freshen them a bit. This was all done rather quickly as to not get kicked out of the hotel, or worse yet, arrested.

We dripped dried as we walked around Beverly Hills in the scorching heat and finally visited my brother's friend at work, unannounced, for about 10 minutes. "We were just in the neighborhood ..."

Then we had to leave for downtown L.A. It was still hot. We took the bus again, only now for added fun, it was rush hour with crowds of tired folks getting on-board to go home.

I was just exhausted. I fell asleep briefly, hoping I wouldn't wake up in Azusa, because we needed to trans-fer. The bus driver was sweet and patient with me since I really had no idea what the hell I was doing even if I was a recent college graduate. He told us what bus to board next, repeatedly saying, "Don't worry when the bus turns left on Olympic." I wouldn't even had known to worry about that, but now I was worried. It was getting late and we still had an evening train to catch. If we missed that, we would probably still be riding the buses around Los Angeles.

I remember dozing in my seat. I had no idea where my mother was, probably sitting behind me or still in a bakery. I didn't even know what day it was. But I knew I was hungry and feeling faint. Then I perked up when I saw the familiar landmark of City Hall and then soon, the downtown train station.

We disembarked and that's when I realized we still had a five hour train trip ahead of us. Sigh. We decided to find a restaurant downtown. Again, like we do what we were doing. We walked around and ended up in Chinatown at a family-owned restaurant that had just closed for lunch and wasn't open yet for dinner. They served us anyway. Just my mom and me in the place. Oh, and the owners, too, sitting across from us at another table, watching us eat. The older daughter was nice, yet curious, asking us how long were we in town? After that bus ride I felt like we had already been in town for a week.

Then it was on the train again to Las Vegas. You know

you have traveled the train a lot when you recognize the porters and conductors, like I did on this train. We had the same conductor that we had during our big Vegas trip when I was suffering from my sinus woes and my brother.

After a few days in Las Vegas, we returned to L.A., not leaving the station for any sidetrips, but just the train to Oakland. Always pretty along the central coast. We stayed in San Francisco a few days and then went to Oregon for my sister's graduation. The train ride there was uneventful. A nice change.

Later we actually drove north to Bellingham, Wash., to help my sister relocate for a new job. I did most of the driving as I was becoming more comfortable with mountainous terrain. It helped that I had a crash course driving mountain roads a few years earlier when my sister let me drive a portion of a trip from Oregon to San Francisco. I asked her if there were any upcoming mountains. I think she said no. She dozed off and the next thing I saw was a 6% downhill grade sign and nothing but the top of the road and blue sky on the horizon. I learned it was not a good idea to brake constantly while driving downhill.

This time I drove us up north where everything was

going smoothly with the exception of me trying to read the mind of a state trooper in Seattle as his car lights were flashing behind me and I was still in his way even after five minutes had passed. Boy, did he give me a look when he drove by. Also along this interstate we discovered the rest stops with cookies and coffee.

We didn't really encounter problems going back to Eugene other than we left Bellingham too late with no motel in mind to spend the night. There were no upcoming road signs with hotels mentioned on them, and very few if any billboards. It was getting darker and all we saw were hills, thick forests and no motels. So of course, we ended up at a rest stop. Better safe than sorry. I didn't mind as there were only the three of us in my sister's Nova. Fewer bodies meant more legroom. Plus there were hot chocolate and cookies!!!

We settled in as best we could for the night, and for some reason shared scary stories. Great. Big Foot was probably listening in the next car. We finally fell asleep and all was well until our car dome light turned on by itself at 3 a.m. Not sure how that happened. Don't want to know. I don't think we slept the rest of the night.

After daybreak and one more hot chocolate, we were on our way, thinking there would be more hills and no place to stop for many, many miles. We were wrong. Just five miles past this rest area was a small town loaded with hotels and restaurants that could give Las Vegas a run for its money. Had we only known.

We said good-bye to my sister a few days later, and my mom and I were off for Detroit. Again on the train. In coach with few supplies like food and snacks.

If you want a gorgeous train ride, you must travel through the Columbia Gorge. Stunning. Then the next day you awake in Glacier National Park in Montana. More beauty. I was really enjoying all of this until it dawned on me that we would still be on this train at least two more days and nights. And this area of the country was flat, pretty, but flat.

I don't know what the deal was with the food, but we never bought meals on the train. Maybe too expensive at the time? Who knows? All we had to eat were plain peanut butter sandwiches and roasted almonds, which I don't like. The food was so dry that I couldn't open my mouth at times. I'm sure my mom enjoyed the break.

I looked on with envy as other passengers gorged on their fancy, pre-planned meals, debating whether they would really miss the other half of that sandwich if they looked away or fell asleep. We may have finally bought a sandwich during a train stop in Williston, N.D. At this point I just wanted off the train. That wasn't going to happen for another two-and-a-half days.

But I was still very grateful for the trip and that it didn't take place in winter.

Chapter Fourteen

Final Thoughts

I am thankful I never experienced food poisoning while traveling. And I eat constantly.

I'm thankful I never lost a rental car in a parking lot. You know, you come outside and forgot what the car looked like. But I did lose my car once in a sea of about 1,000 cars at an airport parking lot. A nice employee helped me by climbing what looked like a fire tower and quickly located my car.

I'm thankful for never being arrested or being jailed while in another country.

I'm thankful when the turbulence isn't as bad as the captain predicted.

I'm very thankful for my dad who helped me overcome my fear of flying.

And I'm most thankful for growing up with a great family who loved to travel, especially on a moment's notice.

Final approach ...

There is nothing more fun than a sudden road trip.

There is nothing more soulful than riding in a train at night and hearing its horn and the ringing bells of a railroad crossing.

There is nothing more relaxing than sipping coffee as you watch the sunset while cruising at 35,000 feet.

And there is no better feeling than going to the airport to pick up a dear friend or loved one. Maybe that also holds true at times for taking them back (myself included).

THE END

"ALL ABOARD!"

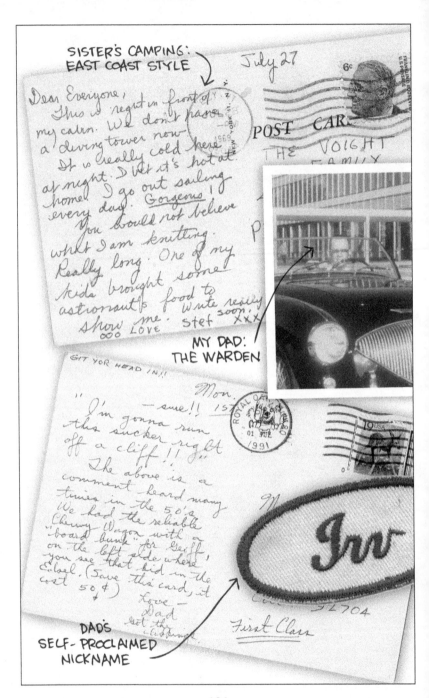

SISTER'S CAMPING: EAST COAST STYLE

July 27

Dear Everyone,
This is right in front of my cabin. We don't have a diving tower now. It is really cold here at night. I bet it's hot at home. I go out sailing every day. Gorgeous!
You would not believe what I am knitting. Really long. One of my kids brought some astronaut's food to show me. Write really soon.
ooo LOVE. Stef xxx

6¢
FRANKLIN ROOSEVELT U.S. POSTAGE
NEW YORK 1969

POST CARD

THE VOIGHT FAMILY

MY DAD: THE WARDEN

GIT YOR HEAD IN!!

"I'm gonna run this sucker right off a cliff!!"
The above is a comment heard many times in the 50's. We had the reliable "Chevy Wagon with a "board bunk" for Geoff, on the left side where you see that kid in the Ethel. (Save this card, it cost 50¢)
Love— Dad got the message.

Mon. — sure!! 15th
ROYAL OAK 01 JUL 1991
10 USA
First Class

Irv
IL704

DADS SELF-PROCLAIMED NICKNAME

130

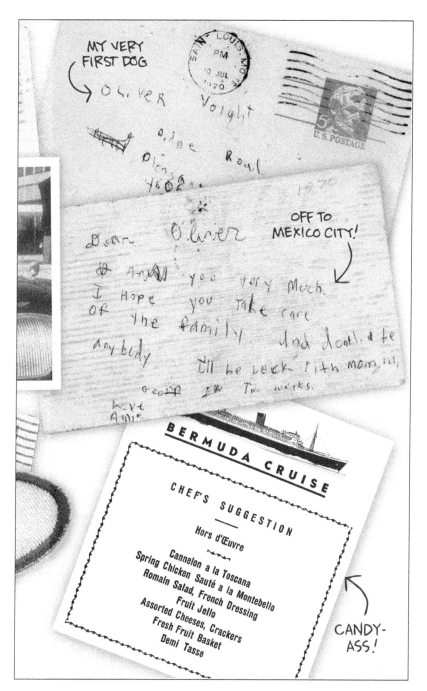

MY VERY
FIRST DOG
→ OLIVER

SAINT LOUIS MO
PM
10 JUL
1970

Oliver Voight
Ridge Road
Y602

U.S. POSTAGE
5¢

1970

Dear Oliver

OFF TO
MEXICO CITY!
↓

I thank you very Much.
I Hope you Take care
of the family. And don't bite
Anybody. I'll be back with mom, rit,

Scott In Two weeks.

love
Amie

BERMUDA CRUISE

CHEF'S SUGGESTION

Hors d'Œuvre
~~~
Cannelon a la Toscana
Spring Chicken Sauté a la Montebello
Romain Salad, French Dressing
Fruit Jello
Assorted Cheeses, Crackers
Fresh Fruit Basket
Demi Tasse

CANDY-
ASS!
↖

131

CPSIA information can be obtained
at www.ICGtesting.com
Printed in the USA
FSHW010510241219
65426FS